CANDICELY

GROW.TRANSFORM.HEAL

Boundaries Without Guilt: A Guided Workbook for Women

Disclaimer
This publication has been created and authored by Candice N. Crowley. It is published and intended for informational and educational purposes only. It is not a substitute for professional mental health treatment, therapy, or medical advice, and does not create a client/therapist relationship.

The author has made every effort to ensure the accuracy and completeness of the information in this workbook. The author assumes no responsibility for errors, omissions, or outcomes resulting from the use of this material.

First published 2026

Published by *Grow.Transform.Heal* Press An Imprint of Candicely | candicely.com

ISBN: 979-8-9959642-0-9

Printed in the United States of America

To the woman reading this —

Thank you. From the bottom of my heart.

You did not have to choose this. You did not have to decide that you were worth the investment of time, honesty, and the kind of self-reflection that this work requires. But you did. And you should feel extremely proud of that.

I created this collection from every conversation, every session, every woman who has crossed my path — in my practice, in my friendships, in my family — quietly bearing far more than was ever hers to hold. I finished it because of women like you, women who are finally ready to choose themselves.

However this found you, through a friend or by some quiet nudge you can't quite explain, I believe that you are ***exactly*** *where you are supposed to be.*

Do the work. Be patient with yourself. And know that every time you choose yourself — even imperfectly, even just a little — you are already doing something revolutionary.

With an abundance of gratitude,

Candice

CANDICELY

GROW.TRANSFORM.HEAL

THIS BODY OF WORK IS DEDICATED ....

First to my Heavenly Father, Who constantly reminds me that my life is not my own and Who used me as a vessel to create this specifically for you ... whoever you are.

And to my supportive husband, who has embraced and encouraged my continued evolution.

And to my adult children, who are on their own journeys and implementing boundaries with us as they figure it out.

And to my Aunt Shivon, whose 2011 passing was in part due to a lack of boundaries.

And to my family of origin, who respects my boundaries.

And to the dynamic women who helped me get this to the finish line.

And to every woman who has suppressed her inner voice to accommodate someone who would never consider accommodating her.

And finally, to every version of myself that said yes when she meant no — this is for her, too. The most revolutionary thing she ever did was choose herself — no explanation, no apology, no asking for permission.

I created this workbook because I've interacted with too many brilliant, capable, loving women, who forgot they were allowed to need something. Women so busy holding everything together for everyone else that they lost the thread back to themselves.

This is me handing it back ... with love and compassion.

— *Candice N. Crowley*

Meet Maya

Maya is the daughter of a woman who never said no to those around her. She watched her mother absorb everything — her father's moods, the emotional demands of friends, and the expectations of family — without complaint. Expressing a need in Maya's childhood home was inconvenient and often led to conflict.

Maya learned, either by words or observations, that a good girl kept the peace, stayed small, and made sure everyone else was comfortable first. Maya carried this into adulthood, without ever questioning whether it was a healthy mindset.

Today, Maya moves through her life quietly accommodating everyone around her — at home, at work, in every room she enters — rarely asked, rarely acknowledged, rarely putting herself first. At work, she takes on more than her share and says nothing. At home, she manages the children, the schedules, the aging parents, and the emotional temperature of every room she walks into. In her relationship, she gives consistently and asks for almost nothing — not because she doesn't have needs, but because she's never trusted that her needs were worth the disruption.

When she imagines saying no — to her colleagues, her mother, her partner, her children — a specific fear arrives before anything else. Not the practical fear of inconvenience. Something more deeply rooted. The fear that if she stops being useful, agreeable, and endlessly available, the people she loves will leave her.

So she always says yes. And she handles it — all of it — with a smile that has become so practiced she sometimes forgets it isn't real. What Maya doesn't yet have is a single person in her life to whom she has told the truth. Not the full truth. Not the version where she admits how depleted she actually is, how long she has been disappearing, how much resentment has been quietly accumulating in the space between who she is and who she pretends to be. She looks completely fine, but she is falling apart.

Maya's story moves through each deeply personal section of this workbook alongside yours. Her past is not your past. But some of what she carried may feel familiar. Notice where it does.

We are all Maya.

This workbook was made with <u>you</u> in mind.

If you've ever said yes when your soul said no, felt guilty for disappointing someone, or found yourself exhausted from giving so much of yourself away ... you are **<u>not</u>** broken — you were taught.

Many women are socialized from a young age to be agreeable, accommodating, and self-sacrificing. Boundaries can feel selfish, unkind, or even scary. This workbook challenges that thought process and helps to build a new one.

> *Daring to set boundaries is about having the courage to love ourselves, even when we risk disappointing others.*
> *— Brené Brown*

HOW TO USE THIS WORKBOOK:

- Move at your own pace ... there is **<u>no</u>** rush.
- Write honestly, even if it feels uncomfortable.
- Return to sections as many times as you need.
- This is for your eyes only — be real with yourself.
- Remove distractions as you engage in this important work.
- Oh ... and maybe keep some tissue on hand.

We're on this journey together. I'm proud of you for getting started!
– *Candice*

PART ONE

Understanding Your Boundary *Patterns*

Before we can change our patterns, we have to see them clearly. This section helps us understand where our current relationship with boundaries began.

1. Your Family's Boundary Blueprint
2. Areas of Depletion
3. People-Pleasing Self-Assessment
4. Resentment as a Boundary Signal

Maya's Moment —

Maya learned early that good girls don't make things harder. In her house, needs were an inconvenience, and being compliant was the price of belonging. She carried that lesson into every relationship she's ever had. Tonight she's at the kitchen sink — dinner still unmade, everyone still needing something — and there is a feeling in her chest she cannot name. She has felt it before. She has never stopped to ask what that feeling is trying to tell her.

Your Family's Boundary Blueprint

The way we learn to handle boundaries — or not handle them — starts in childhood. Reflect on the messages you received growing up.

REFLECTION

Growing up, what did you observe about how the adults in your life said no, asked for space, or communicated their needs?

Whose needs were prioritized in your family, and what did that teach you about your own?

What happened in your home when someone expressed a boundary or disagreed?

Let's Check In

As women, we wear a million hats, showing up as everything, to everyone ... all. the. time. It is imperative that we pause to check in with ourselves, assessing how we feel across all of our life domains, so that we can make adjustments.

In each life domain below, use the box in the corner to identify how you currently feel: Drained (D), Energized (E), or in the Middle (M). Then, write a couple of thoughts about why you feel the way you do.

Romantic Relationships
Emotionally Safe, Unsupported

____

____

Work
Satisfied, Unfulfilled, Stressed

____

____

Social Relationships
Valuable, Burdensome, Obligatory

____

____

Time & Personal Space
Overcommitted, Stretched, Restless

____

____

Family Relationships
Tense, Close, Estranged

____

____

Parenting, or if N/A ___________
N/A Ex: Spirituality, Personal Growth

____

____

REFLECTION

Which area surprised you most?

____

Which one do you want to change first?

____

PART ONE

People-Pleasing Self-Assessment

In many families, the unspoken rules for young girls were clear: Be agreeable, don't make waves, put others first, and above all, don't be difficult. This origin leads to a life of people-pleasing.

Read each statement and write in the box how often it feels true for you:
Rarely (R), Sometimes (S), Often (O), or Almost Always (A).

☐ 1. I say yes to requests even when I want to say no.

☐ 2. I feel anxious when I think someone might be upset with me.

☐ 3. I apologize frequently, even when I haven't done anything wrong.

☐ 4. I struggle to ask for help because I don't want to be a burden.

☐ 5. I minimize my own feelings to avoid conflict.

☐ 6. I feel responsible for making sure everyone around me is comfortable.

☐ 7. I agree with people even when I privately disagree.

☐ 8. I feel guilty when I spend time or money on myself.

☐ 9. I have a hard time expressing needs or preferences in relationships.

☐ 10. I feel more comfortable giving than receiving.

Note: If you have mostly "R"s then you're good on this topic!

SURVEY SAYS ...

Answer	Total
R	
S	
O	
A	

REFLECTION

Look at where your "Often" and "Almost Always" answers cluster. What do they tell you about where people-pleasing shows up most in your life?

PART ONE

Resentment as a Boundary Signal

Resentment is one of the most important emotions we can learn to listen to. It is not a character flaw. It is not pettiness. It is our internal alarm system telling us that something has been taken — or given away — that we didn't truly have **OR** want to offer.

REFLECTION

Toward whom or what in your life are you currently carrying resentment?

Write Above

Write Above

When you trace that resentment back, what boundary was crossed or never set?

What would you have needed to say or do differently in that situation?

What does this resentment want you to do differently from here?

Brené Brown writes that resentment is almost always about unmet needs and unexpressed limits. When you feel resentful toward someone, it is rarely because they are a bad person. It is usually because you have been saying yes when you meant no — and a part of you knows it.

Recap & Next Steps:
Understanding Your Boundary Patterns

What We Explored:

- Where your relationship with boundaries began — the family patterns and unspoken rules that shaped you
- How people-pleasing shows up in your life
- Where you feel most depleted and what that depletion is telling you
- How resentment functions as a signal — not a character flaw

What Maya Learned: Maya stood at that sink and finally let herself feel the stone in her chest instead of pushing past it. She didn't have answers yet. But for the first time, she stopped pretending the feeling wasn't there.

Your Biggest Takeaway(s): ______________________

____

____

Your Next Steps:

1. Share what you discovered with someone you trust — a friend, a therapist, or someone doing this work alongside you. Saying it out loud makes it real in a way that staying in your head never will.
2. If you felt resistance or numbness moving through this section, sit with one question before you move on: What am I afraid I might find if I look more closely? Write your answer honestly — even if it is uncomfortable.

PART TWO

The Guilt and Fear Behind Saying *No!*

If setting boundaries were easy, you wouldn't need this workbook. The reason it's difficult isn't weakness — it's wiring, as many women have been socially conditioned since childhood to associate saying no with being selfish, unkind, or unlovable. This section is the emotional core of the work.

1. Why Saying No Feels So Hard
2. The Good-Girl Conditioning
3. Reframing Guilt
4. Building Self-Trust

Maya's Moment —

Maya almost says no on a Tuesday. She has the word. She feels it clearly. And yet says yes anyway. Sitting at her desk afterward, she remembers something older than the moment — a girl who learned that love was something you earned by never being too much. The guilt feels like a verdict. She is only just beginning to wonder if it's lying to her.

PART TWO

Why Saying No Feels So Hard

Before we can change our behavior, we have to understand what's driving it. For most of us, it comes down to a handful of **core fears:**

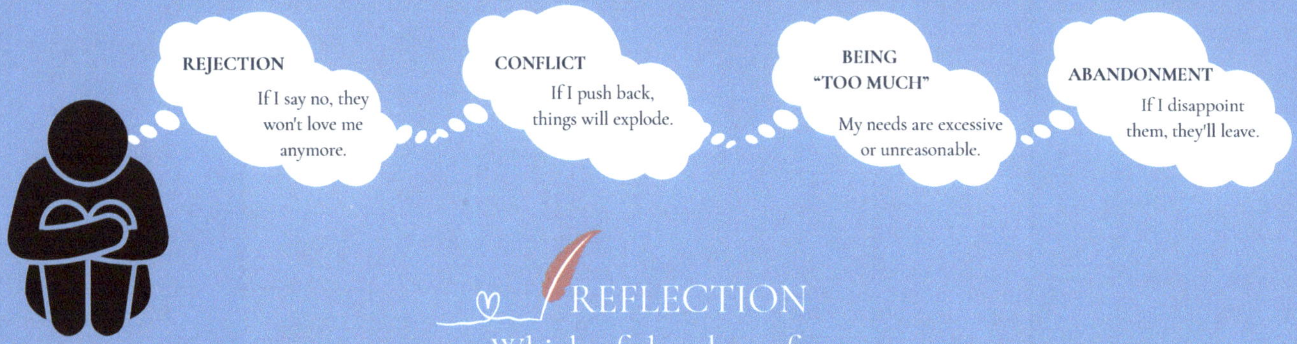

REFLECTION

Which of the above fears resonate most with you?

Write Above

Write Above

What do you believe will happen if you say no to someone important to you?

Has that fear ever come true? What actually happened?

Where did you first learn that having boundaries was dangerous or wrong?

PART TWO

The Good-Girl Conditioning

Being taught to be nice, be helpful, be accommodating, share everything, and make sure everyone is happy, is how good-girl conditioning is birthed. It shows up in adulthood as chronic over-giving, difficulty with self-advocacy, and a profound discomfort with being perceived as selfish or demanding.

REFLECTION

How does the "good girl" show up in your life today?

We feel guilty for resting when there's still something to be done.

We are the first to say yes and the last to admit we are underwater.

We apologize for asking for what we need.

We prioritize everyone's comfort above our own.

Growing up, what did you gain by going along — approval, peace, love, safety? How did receiving those things shape the woman you became?

What happened when you pushed back or disagreed growing up — silence, anger, withdrawal, punishment? What did you learn to do instead?

In which relationship(s) do you still feel pressure to be "good" at the expense of being honest?

- ☐ *Romantic Relationship(s)*
- ☐ *Social Relationships*
- ☐ *Work/Professional Relationships*
- ☐ *Family of Origin Relationships*
- ☐ *Other:* ____________

Reframing Guilt

Guilt is one of the most powerful forces keeping us from setting boundaries. It's important to understand that guilt is a feeling, not a verdict. Guilt tells us that we've done something wrong. But when the "wrong thing" is simply taking care of ourselves, honoring our needs, or saying no to something we couldn't give, guilt is lying to us.

REFLECTION

Think of a recent time you felt guilty for saying no or putting yourself first. What story were you telling yourself?

Healthy guilt *shows up when you've genuinely acted against your values, when you've hurt someone, broken a commitment, or been unkind. This guilt is useful. It points you toward repair.*

Conditioned guilt *shows up simply because you've prioritized yourself, disappointed someone, or broken an unspoken rule about how "good girls" are supposed to behave. This guilt is not useful.*

What would you tell a close friend who felt guilty for the same thing?

What would it mean for you to feel guilt and hold your boundary anyway?

Building Self-Trust

At the root of most boundary struggles is a deficit of self-trust. When we've spent years overriding our own instincts, suppressing our needs, and deferring to others' comfort, we lose touch with our inner knowing. Rebuilding self-trust is not a dramatic event. It happens in small moments — every time you listen to what your body is telling you, every time you honor a need instead of dismissing it, every time you say no and survive the discomfort that follows.

REFLECTION

Describe a time when you ignored your gut and later wished you hadn't.

What does your body feel like when something is wrong, when a boundary is being pushed?

Write a few sentences to yourself as if you were your own most trusted advisor. What do you need to hear?

What small act of self-trust can you commit to this week?

Recap & Next Steps:

The Guilt and Fear Behind Saying No!

What We Explored:

- The core fears that live underneath your people-pleasing — rejection, conflict, abandonment, being too much
- Where good-girl conditioning came from and how it shows up in your adult life
- The difference between healthy guilt and conditioned guilt — and how to tell them apart
- How to begin rebuilding self-trust, one small moment at a time

What Maya Learned: Maya realized the guilt she felt about saying no wasn't evidence that she had done something wrong. It was a reflex — practiced so many times it felt like truth. She couldn't unlearn it overnight. But she could start questioning it.

Your Biggest Takeaway(s): ____________________

____

____

Your Next Steps:

1. Share what you discovered with someone you trust — a friend, a therapist, or someone doing this work alongside you. Saying it out loud makes it real in a way that staying in your head never will.
2. The next time guilt arrives, after you say no or choose yourself, pause before acting on it. Ask yourself: Is this healthy guilt or conditioned guilt? You do not have to answer perfectly. Just ask the question.

PART THREE

How to Set *Boundaries*

We now understand why boundaries haven't existed and the impact of that. Now, let's look at how to put boundaries in place.

1. The Four Types of Boundaries
2. Three-Step Framework
3. Scripts for Hard Conversations
4. When Someone Pushes Back

Maya's Moment —

On Saturday morning, Maya sits down across from her partner and says the thing she has been rehearsing for two weeks. Not perfectly. Voice unsteady. Almost apologizing twice. But she says it plainly, without justification. And when the silence comes, she does not fill it. Warm and firm at the same time. Both things, together, for the first time.

The Four Types of Boundaries

Boundaries exist in every area of our lives, not just in dramatic confrontations. Understanding the different types can help us identify where we need the most attention.

Physical

Physical boundaries *govern your body, your personal space, and your physical environment. They include things like not wanting to be touched in certain ways, needing alone time, or requiring a workspace that feels calm and ordered.*

Emotional

Emotional boundaries *protect your inner world. They involve not taking responsibility for others' feelings, not absorbing other people's stress, and not allowing someone to speak to you with cruelty or contempt.*

Time

Time boundaries *are about how you allocate one of your most finite resources. They include saying no to commitments that deplete you, protecting time for rest and restoration, and not being available 24 hours a day for everyone who wants your attention.*

Digital

Digital boundaries *are increasingly important in a hyperconnected world. They include not responding to messages at all hours, not engaging in draining conversations online, and protecting your mental space from constant input.*

REFLECTION

Which of the four types feels most difficult for you to protect? Why?

"No" is a complete sentence. — Annie Lamott

Let's Check In

In each life domain below, use the box in the corner to identify which boundary is being depleted: Physical (P), Emotional (E), Time (T), or Digital (D). Then, write a couple of thoughts about why you feel the way you do.

Romantic Relationships
Emotionally Safe, Unsupported

____

____

Work
Satisfied, Unfulfilled, Stressed

____

____

Social Relationships
Valuable, Burdensome, Obligatory

____

____

Time & Personal Space
Overcommitted, Stretched, Restless

____

____

Family Relationships
Tense, Close, Estranged

____

____

Parenting, or if N/A __________
N/A Ex: Spirituality, Personal Growth

____

____

REFLECTION

What is one small boundary you could set this week in your most depleted area?

____

____

A Simple Three-Step Framework

Setting a boundary doesn't have to be confrontational. It can be calm, clear, and even kind. Here is a simple framework you can return to again and again.

1

Name what you need.
Get clear within yourself first. What do you actually need in this situation? Not what seems reasonable, not what you think you're allowed to want, what do you genuinely need?

→

2

Say it simply.
You do not need to build a case. You do not need to justify, defend, or apologize. A boundary stated plainly is enough. "I'm not able to do that." "I need some time to myself tonight." "That doesn't work for me."

→

3

Hold it with compassion.
You can be firm and warm at the same time. Holding a boundary does not require coldness, anger, or distance. It just requires consistency. If someone pushes back, you don't need to re-explain — you can simply repeat your boundary calmly.

REFLECTION

Think of a boundary you've been wanting to set. What you would say using the three steps above?

What feels hardest about Step 2?

What does Step 3 look like for you?

PART THREE

Scripts for Hard Conversations

Sometimes we know what we need to say, we just don't know how to say it. Here are ready-to-use scripts for the relationships where boundaries tend to be hardest.

With a partner:

"I love you, and I need to tell you something that's been hard for me to say. When [X] happens, I feel [Y]. I need [Z]. I'm not saying this to start a fight — I'm saying it because I want us to be closer."

With a parent or in-law:

"I appreciate how much you care. And I need to ask that [X]. This isn't about loving you less — it's about what I need to feel okay."

With a friend:

"I value our friendship so much, and I've been realizing I need to be more honest with you. I can't [X] anymore. I hope you can understand."

With a co-worker or manager:

"I want to make sure I'm doing my best work. To do that, I need to be realistic about my capacity. I'm not able to take on [X] right now, but here's what I can do ..."

When someone pushes back:

"I understand this might be disappointing. My answer is still no."

When you don't have words yet:

"I need some time to think about that. I'll get back to you."

PART THREE

Practice Makes Perfect

Spend some time thinking about the scripts and how you can apply them to different areas in your life.

REFLECTION

Who do you most need a script for right now?

Write Above

Write Above

Is there a conversation you've been avoiding? Write out what you would say using the scripts.

What makes that conversation feel risky? What might be possible on the other side of it?

When Someone Pushes Back

One of the biggest reasons we abandon our boundaries is that we're not prepared for pushback. When someone reacts with hurt, anger, guilt-tripping, or silence, it can feel like confirmation that we did something wrong. **It isn't.** When someone pushes back on a boundary, they are expressing their disappointment, which is valid. But their disappointment is **not** a signal that your boundary was wrong. It is simply information about how they feel. You are **not responsible** for managing that feeling for them.

Common Pushback Tactics & Responses

Guilt—tripping:
"I can't believe you'd do this to me."

→ "I'm sorry you're hurting. My answer hasn't changed."

Minimizing:
"You're so sensitive. I was just joking."

→ "Maybe so. But it still affected me, and I need it to stop."

Negotiating:
"What if we just ... ?"

→ "I hear you. This is what works for me."

Silence or withdrawal:

→ You do not need to chase. Give them space and trust that the relationship can survive honesty.

REFLECTION

Which pushback tactic is hardest for you to withstand? Why?

What do you typically do when someone reacts badly to your no?

What would it look like to stay calm and hold your ground in that moment?

PART THREE

Recap & Next Steps:

How to Set Boundaries

What We Explored:

- The four types of boundaries — physical, emotional, time, and digital — and where yours need the most attention
- A simple three-step framework for setting a boundary clearly and with compassion
- Scripts for the hardest conversations with partners, family, friends, and colleagues
- How to stay grounded when someone pushes back

What Maya Learned: Maya sat down at that table and said the thing she had been rehearsing for two weeks. It wasn't perfect. But it was honest. And she stayed in the silence afterward without filling it — which was its own kind of victory.

Your Biggest Takeaway(s): ______________________

____

____

Your Next Steps:

1. Share what you discovered with someone you trust — a friend, a therapist, or someone doing this work alongside you. Saying it out loud makes it real in a way that staying in your head never will.
2. Go back to the pushback scripts and choose the ones that feel most useful for what you typically experience. Write them on a separate piece of paper or a note in your phone, somewhere you will see them before the conversations happen.

PART FOUR

Holding *Your* Boundaries

You set the boundary. It felt good — brave, even. And then the guilt crept in. Or they looked hurt. Or things got awkward. And slowly, quietly, you undid it. This final section focuses on how to maintain your boundaries.

1. Why We Abandon Our Boundaries
2. Building a Support System
3. Self-Compassion as a Boundary Tool
4. Your Ongoing Practice

Maya's Moment —

Three months later, Maya is back at the kitchen sink. She caved twice this month. She noticed. She didn't punish herself. Not everything has changed. But the stone in her chest is lighter. She is still here — still present in her own life — learning, one imperfect moment at a time, to stay.

Let's Check In

Below are common reasons we abandon our boundaries. In which life domain(s) have you found yourself abandoning your boundaries for any of these reasons? Check all that apply.

The other person's distress feels unbearable to witness.

- ☐ Romantic Relationship(s)
- ☐ Social Relationships
- ☐ Work/Professional Relationships
- ☐ Family Relationships
- ☐ Other: ________________

The silence or tension feels like punishment.

- ☐ Romantic Relationship(s)
- ☐ Social Relationships
- ☐ Work/Professional Relationships
- ☐ Family Relationships
- ☐ Other: ________________

I begin to doubt whether my boundary is reasonable.

- ☐ Romantic Relationship(s)
- ☐ Social Relationships
- ☐ Work/Professional Relationships
- ☐ Family Relationships
- ☐ Other: ________________

I want to restore harmony as quickly as possible.

- ☐ Romantic Relationship(s)
- ☐ Social Relationships
- ☐ Work/Professional Relationships
- ☐ Family Relationships
- ☐ Other: ________________

I feel selfish for holding firm.

- ☐ Romantic Relationship(s)
- ☐ Social Relationships
- ☐ Work/Professional Relationships
- ☐ Family Relationships
- ☐ Other: ________________

PART FOUR

Why We Abandon Our Boundaries

Caving after setting a boundary is one of the most common experiences we have when we're learning to set boundaries for the first time. And it makes complete sense — we're changing a pattern that has been in place for years, possibly decades. The pullback toward the old way is strong. Here's what's important to understand: Caving does not mean we failed, it means we're human. The goal is not perfection, it is awareness. Every time we notice that we've caved, we have an opportunity to understand why, and to choose differently next time.

REFLECTION

Think of a recent time you set a boundary and then backed down. What happened in that moment?

What were you most afraid of if you had held it?

What would you do differently now?

What does it cost you — repeatedly abandoning your boundaries?

PART FOUR

Building a Support System

Changing deeply ingrained patterns is not something you have to do alone. In fact, trying to do it alone is one of the things that makes it hardest. A support system for this work might look like ...

A therapist or counselor
who can help you process the deeper emotional roots of your people-pleasing patterns and hold space for the harder feelings that come up.

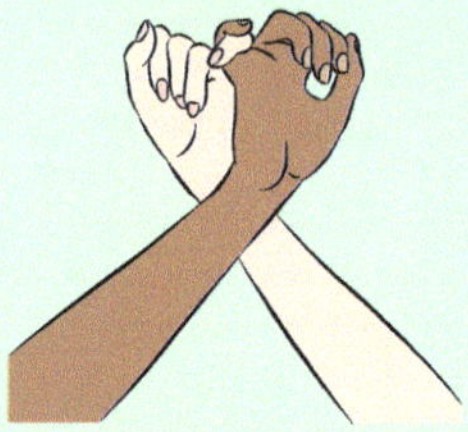

A trusted friend
who is also doing her own growth work, someone you can be honest with about the messy middle of change.

A community of women
who understand this struggle — whether that's a group program, a support group, or an online community built around these themes.

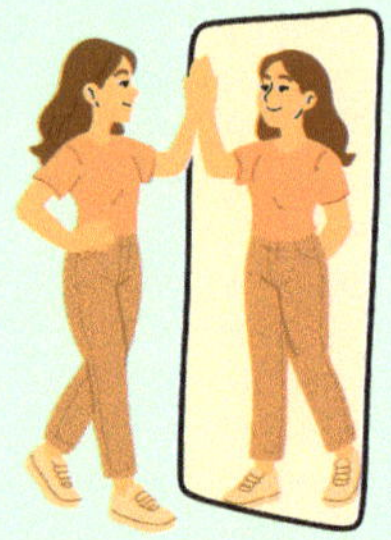

Yourself *—*
your own journaling practice, your own compassionate self-talk, your own commitment to noticing and naming what you feel before you override it.

REFLECTION

Who in your life currently supports your growth?

Write Above

Write Above

Who in your life actively — even if unintentionally — makes it harder for you to hold boundaries?

What kind of support do you most need right now that you don't currently have?

What is one step you could take this week to build more support around this work?

PART FOUR

Self-Compassion as a Boundary Tool

The more compassion we have for ourselves, the easier it becomes to hold boundaries. When we are harsh with ourselves — expecting perfection, berating ourselves for caving, or feeling ashamed for struggling — we become less equipped to set and hold boundaries. Shame drives us back into people-pleasing because we feel unworthy of the very things we're trying to claim. Self-compassion is not self-indulgence — it is the foundation of sustainable change. It means treating ourselves with the same gentleness we would offer a dear friend who was doing something hard, imperfect, and brave.

"This is hard. Of course it's hard. I'm learning something new."

"I am doing the best I can with what I know right now."

"I caved today. That's okay. I noticed it, and I'll try again."

REFLECTION

How do you typically speak to yourself when you make a mistake or fall back into old patterns?

What would you say to a close friend in the same situation?

PART FOUR

Practice Makes Perfect

Spend some time thinking about how you talk to yourself versus how you'd talk to a friend.

REFLECTION

Write yourself a short, compassionate note about where you are right now in this journey.

What does your inner critic most need to hear from you today?

Your Ongoing Practice

Setting and holding boundaries is not a destination — it is a practice. As part of that practice, it's important to understand what boundaries are and what they are not. Boundaries are not walls. They are not punishment. They are not selfish, unkind, or permanent. They are not ultimatums designed to control someone else's behavior. They are doors — ones you control. They are honest communication. They are the language of self-respect. And they are one of the most loving things you can offer any relationship, including the one you have with yourself.

Boundaries ARE

- Doors you control
- Honest communication
- Self-aware and sustainable
- Statements about your own behavior
- The foundation of real intimacy
- Living and evolving

Boundaries Are **NOT**

- Walls that shut people out
- Punishment for bad behavior
- Selfish or self-centered
- Ultimatums or threats
- Unkind or cold
- Fixed and permanent

Which misconception about boundaries have you believed most strongly?

____

____

____

____

Have you ever confused having boundaries with being unkind or difficult? What did that cost you?

____

____

____

____

What would change in your relationships if the people around you understood boundaries the way you now do?

____

____

What is one boundary you are committing to set or hold in the next 30 days?

____

Recap & Next Steps:
Holding Your Boundaries

What We Explored:

- Why we cave — and what it actually costs us when we do
- How to build a support system that makes holding boundaries sustainable
- Self-compassion as a practice, not a reward for getting it right
- What an ongoing boundary practice looks like in real, imperfect life
- What boundaries are and what they are **not**

What Maya Learned: Maya caved twice. She noticed. She didn't punish herself. She came back. That — more than any perfect moment — is what the practice actually looks like.

Your Biggest Takeaway(s): ______________________

____

____

Your Next Steps:

1. On the next page, write yourself a letter — not about who you want to become, but about who you already are. What has this work asked of you? What have you shown up for? What are you proud of even if nobody else saw it? Include your own definition of what a boundary means to you and how you'll apply it to your life. Read it back to yourself the next time you cave and need to find your way back
2. Share your letter with someone you trust — a friend, a therapist, or someone doing this work alongside you. Ask them to hold you accountable to the work you've done and to remind you to come back to it the next time you fall you back into old patterns.

A Letter To Myself

DATE:

DEAR

LOVE,

Complete this sentence:
"The woman I am becoming is someone who ... "

FINAL THOUGHTS

Maya's Final Moment —

Maya catches herself at 11pm — lying in bed obsessing over everything she did wrong today, finding herself guilty on every count. Nobody is doing this to her. She is doing it to herself — with more consistency than anyone in her life ever has. It occurs to her quietly in the dark that she has spent all this time learning to protect herself from the world and has not once thought to protect herself from this. She does not fix it tonight. But she notices it. And noticing, she is learning, is always where it begins.

Things to Remember

Check in with your body.
It knows before your mind does when something isn't right. Tightness, exhaustion, a knot that won't go away — these are signals worth listening to.

Notice resentment early.
The moment it begins to build, ask yourself — what boundary have I not set or not held that allowed this?

Repair without abandoning yourself.
If you handle something poorly, repair it. But repair the relationship without giving up the boundary that needed to be there.

Celebrate the small wins.
Every no. Every held ground. Every moment you chose yourself without apologizing — that is worth noticing.

Use your affirmation cards.
One card each morning is a daily reminder of what has always been true about you. Let the deck carry the work into your everyday life.

A Note on *Internal Boundaries*
External boundaries protect you from the world. Internal boundaries protect you from yourself — the agreements you make about how you will treat yourself regardless of what anyone else does.

- *I will not speak to myself in ways I would never speak to someone I love*
- *I will honor my commitments to myself with the same firmness I give to others*
- *I will protect my rest, my restoration, and my care — these are not negotiable*
- *I will catch my inner critic and choose not to follow it into the spiral*

Both kinds of boundaries require practice. Both are worth holding.

REFLECTION

What is one internal boundary you have never set but know, if you are being honest with yourself, that you need?

A Promise to *Yourself*

Congratulations!!

You've done the hard work of being introspective and honest with yourself. Now, seal it with a commitment — not to be perfect, but to make ***continuous*** progress.

"

I, _________________, commit to honoring **my** needs, communicating **my** boundaries with compassion, and **releasing the guilt** that has kept me small. I **deserve** relationships built on mutual respect, and I am allowed to require that. I will **maintain my boundaries**, because my life depends on it.

SIGNATURE DATE

Thank you for trusting me with this part of your journey. It has been an honor to be in these pages with you.

— *Candice N. Crowley*

CANDICELY

GROW.TRANSFORM.HEAL

You Did Something Brave

Most people buy workbooks and leave them on a shelf. You opened this one. You wrote in it. You stayed with it. That is not nothing. That is the beginning of everything.

If You Want to Go Further

This workbook was designed to open a door. What's on the other side of that door — the deeper patterns, the relationships that need honest conversations, the version of yourself you are still becoming — that work is worth doing with the support of a therapist, close friend, or group of trusted women.

The Companion Deck

If you haven't already gotten one, the *"I Am Allowed"* affirmation card deck was designed to sit alongside this workbook as your daily practice. Thirty cards. Four chapters. Cards to carry the work into your daily life.

Available at candicely.com.

If you'd like to share a testimonial or provide feedback about your experience doing this work, send to: hello@candicely.com.

In your message please indicate whether this is between us or if you want to share it with other women.

Here is how we can work together:

Individual Therapy

I offer individual therapy for women navigating people-pleasing, self-worth, relational boundaries, and identity. My approach is warm, direct, and deeply collaborative — I will never tell you what to do, but I will help you figure out what you actually want.

Currently accepting clients in Ohio. Telehealth available.

Speaking & Panel Appearances

I speak on women's mental health, boundary work, burnout, and self-worth for corporate wellness events, conferences, faith communities, and women's organizations. If you are looking for a speaker who combines clinical expertise with real talk and genuine warmth, let's connect.

Let's Connect
Candice N. Crowley, LPCC
candicely.com hello@candicely.com

www.ingramcontent.com/pod-product-compliance
Lightning Source LLC
LaVergne TN
LVHW070956210926
848482LV00002B/224